Bible-based activities to strengthen Christian values

Copyright ©1994 David C. Cook Publishing Co. Printed in the United States of America.

All puzzles and Bible activities are based on the NIV.

Scripture taken from the Holy Bible, New International Version, Copyright ©1973, 1978, 1984 International Bible Society. Used by permission of Zondervan Bible Publishers.

ISBN: 0-7814-5089-6

Edited by Debbie Bible
Book Design by Jack Rogers
Cover Illustration by Corbin Hillam
Interior Illustrations by Barbara Todd & Corbin Hillam

TABLE OF CONTENTS

Introduction for Adult Friends of Children 3-4
What Is Being Cooperative? 5
The Bible Tells about Being Cooperative
    Jethro Gives Moses a Plan 6-7
Working Together on a Mural 8
A Cooperative Stop and Think 9
A Cooperative Class Project 10
A Three-person Drawing 11
Hidden Words about Cooperation 12
A People Search 13
How Many Ways to be Cooperative? 14
A Cooperative Popcorn Party 15
Working Together Everywhere 16
What Do You Think about Cooperating? 17
The Bible Tells about Being Cooperative
    The Believers Share Responsibilities 18-19
Put Yourself in This Maze 20
It's Great to Cooperate 21
Be a Cooperative Cryptographer 22
The Value of Being Cooperative 23

What Is Being Humble? 24
The Bible Tells about Being Humble
    A Humble Centurion Believes in Jesus 25-27
Puppets for a Play about Being Humble 28-29
The Centurion Is Humble
    A Puppet Play based on Matthew 7:1-10 30
God Helps the Humble 31
God Loves Everyone the Same 32
A Humble Person 33
A Maze about Being Humble 34
Haughty or Humble? 35
The Bible Tells about Being Humble
    John the Baptist and Jesus 36-37
A Bible Verse about Being Humble 38
John the Baptist Bookmark 39
Willing to Be Humble 40
Think about Others 41
The Value of Being Humble 42
Value Builders Series Index 43-48

COOPERATIVE & HUMBLE

INTRODUCTION FOR ADULT FRIENDS OF CHILDREN
(Parents, Teachers, and Other Friends of Children)

Values. What are they? How do we acquire them? Can we change them?

"Values" is a popular term, usually meaning *the standard that governs how one acts and conducts one's life.* Our personal standards, or values, are learned and adapted, possibly changed and relearned, over a lifetime of experiences and influences.

Children begin acquiring personal values at birth. As parents, teachers, and other adults who love children, we are concerned that they are learning worthwhile values, rather than being randomly influenced by everything around them. By God's design, we cannot control the process of acquiring values, but we can influence the process in a variety of ways. Our consistent modeling of biblical values is a vital influence, but children must also be encouraged to talk about specific values and be aware of these values in action in themselves and others.

These biblical values are God's values. He has established His standards to help us know how to live our lives and how we are to treat other people. Our goal is to have these biblical values be a part of each child's experience.

A value becomes one's own when a person chooses to act on that value consistently. Saying that we hold to the value of honesty, yet bending the truth or telling a lie when pressured is a contradiction.

Providing opportunities for children to investigate a specific value, identifying with people in the Bible who have that value, and trying to put it into practice in real life situations will help strengthen the value in the lives of the children and reinforce its importance. The purpose of the Value Builders Series is to provide such opportunities.

This book in the Value Builders Series focuses on **being cooperative** and **being humble**. Being cooperative is defined as *being willing to do things with others, either playing or working together.* Moses and Jethro devised a cooperative plan to help the Israelites in their day to day business. Another biblical example of cooperation is the people in the early Church, as they selected deacons and helped each other whenever it was needed.

Being humble is *knowing you are not better than other people.* John the Baptist and the centurion are biblical examples of humility. These respected men, each with a sphere of influence, showed respect and honor to Christ and humility toward others.

The Value Builders Series provides Bible story activities, craft activities, and life application activities that focus on specific biblical values. These books can be used by children working alone, or the pages can be reproduced and used in a classroom setting.

In a classroom setting, this book could be used to supplement curriculum that you are using, or it can be used as a curriculum itself in a 30-55 minute period. Each page is coded at the bottom to suggest where it might fit in a teaching session. The codes are as follows:

🔓 = Definition page

📖 = Bible Story page

✒ = Craft page

👥 = Life Application page

Some suggestions for using the materials in this book in a 30-55 minute period are:

5-10 minutes:	Introduce the value and discuss the definition. Use pages entitled, "What Is Being Cooperative?" or "What Is Being Humble?"
10-15 minutes:	Present one of the Bible stories using appropriate pages. Encourage the children to describe what it might have been like to be in that situation and what other things could have happened.
10-20 minutes:	Choose life application activity pages or craft activities that are appropriate to the children in your class. Design some group applications for the pages you have chosen.
5-10 minutes:	To conclude, use the page entitled, "The Value of Being Cooperative," or "The Value of Being Humble" and encourage the children to make a commitment to focus on this value for the next few days or weeks. Pray for God's help to guide the children as they learn to live by His standards.

WHAT IS BEING COOPERATIVE?

BEING COOPERATIVE IS . . .
being willing to work together with others.

I think being cooperative also means _____

_____

Here are some words about being cooperative.
✂ **Cut them out then ask a friend to cooperate with you as you put them together.**

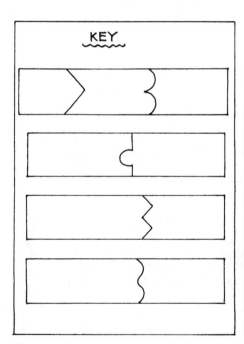

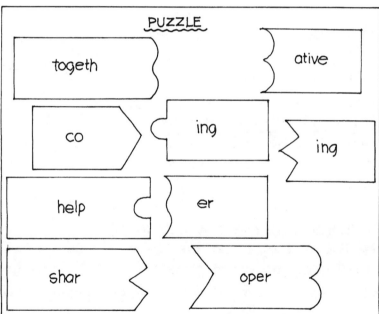

KEY

PUZZLE

togeth
ative
co
ing
ing
help
er
shar
oper

Being cooperative is important to me.

When I willingly work together with others, then being cooperative becomes one of my values.

Name _____

Date _____

God's values are the STANDARD to help me know how to live my life and treat other people

Jethro Gives Moses a Plan

Exodus 18:1-24

Now Jethro, the priest of Midian and father-in-law of Moses, heard of everything God had done for Moses and for his people Israel, and how the LORD had brought Israel out of Egypt. . . .

Jethro, Moses' father-in-law, together with Moses' sons and wife, came to him in the desert, where he was camped near the mountain of God. . . .

When his father-in-law saw all that Moses was doing for the people, he said, "What is this you are doing for the people? Why do you alone sit as judge, while all these people stand around you from morning till evening?"

Moses answered him, "Because the people come to me to seek God's will. Whenever they have a dispute, it is brought to me, and I decide between the parties and inform them of God's decrees and laws."

(Read the rest of this story on page 7)

There may have been hundreds of people coming to Moses every day for help! He was busy from morning to night, helping people decide what to do. This was too much for Moses to do.

✎ **Underline these words in the Bible story then use them to do the crossword puzzle:**

father-in-law   Jethro   decrees   parties   dispute   judge

ACROSS
1. Jethro was this to Moses
5. someone who helps people decide what to do when they have problems
6. Moses' wife's dad

DOWN
2. groups of people
3. laws
4. not agreeing about something

THE BIBLE TELLS ABOUT BEING COOPERATIVE

Jethro Gives Moses a Plan

(Exodus 18:1-24 continued from page 6)

Moses' father-in-law replied, "What you are doing is not good. You and these people who come to you will only wear yourselves out. The work is too heavy for you; you cannot handle it alone. Listen now to me and I will give you some advice, and may God be with you. You must be the people's representative before God and bring their disputes to him. Teach them the decrees and laws, and show them the way to live and the duties they are to perform.

"But select capable men from all the people—men who fear God, trustworthy men who hate dishonest gain—and appoint them as officials. . . . That will make your load lighter, because they will share it with you. . . ." Moses listened to his father-in-law and did everything he said.

Who said?

✎ **Look in the Bible story and then write, in the blanks, the names of the people who said each quote. Draw a picture to illustrate what was happening in each situation.**

1. _____
said to

_____,
"Why are you the only one who is helping the people work out their disputes?"

2. "The people want help to know God's way to do things." said

_____

3. "What you are doing is not right." said

_____ .

4. _____
said to

_____

"If you have more judges cooperating with you, your job will be easier."

WORKING TOGETHER ON A MURAL

✏️ **Make a mosaic mural with a friend.**

I'D LIKE TO BE A PART OF THIS PROJECT. DON'T YOU THINK I'D FIT IN WELL?

YOU'D MAKE A GREAT MOUNTAIN. I'LL GLUE YOU IN.

You need:

- ☐ Construction paper
- ☐ Glue
- ☐ Mural paper (check the local newspaper for free end rolls from the press)
- ☐ Markers

✂️ **To make a mosaic mural follow these directions:**

1. Ask a friend to help you create a mural of Moses, Jethro, and the other people cooperating. You may use the picture below for ideas.
2. Draw a picture.
3. Decide which colors of paper to use on each section.
4. Tear the paper into pieces smaller than one-inch square.
5. Spread glue into each section of the picture and put the torn paper pieces on the glue. Carefully tear and fit the paper to the details of the picture.
6. Allow time for the glue to dry, then hang your picture up for all to see.

A COOPERATIVE STOP AND THINK

When you are working on a project with someone remember these three tips:

STOP and look at the other person.

THINK about what it would be like to be in his/her place.

ACT in a way that helps to build cooperation.

What do you think these cooperative people might do or say? ✎ **Write your ideas on the lines.**

1. You and Kevin are working on a science project. Kevin just broke the main part! Oh, no!

STOP! Think about Kevin.
THINK! How would you feel if you were in Kevin's place?
ACT! What will you do?

_____

_____

_____

2. Your Sunday school class is talking about how to fix up the classroom. Terry is new in the class and you notice he is off by himself.

STOP! Think about Terry.
THINK! How would you feel if you were in Terry's place?
ACT! What will you do?

_____

_____

_____

A COOPERATIVE CLASS PROJECT

At the Brownsville Church, the Sunday school is planning a dessert party for the senior citizens in the neighborhood around the church. Jane, Larry, Teresa, and David are in a class planning to bake cookies. ✎ **To find out who is doing what, where follow these directions:**

1. Find each person's house and write his or her name just above the house on the map.

CLUES:

A. Jane lives in a one story house with four windows

B. David's house is two stories high with a weather vane

C. Larry's house has three windows and a double front door

D. Teresa's house has a cupola

2. Fill in the blanks:

"Let's get together on Saturday at my house. It's the one with three windows," said _____.

"I'll bring the flour and the sugar. I'll leave my one story house with four windows at one o'clock." said _____.

"I'll watch for you from my cupola. I'll bring some eggs," said _____.

WHAT'S A CUPOLA?   HERE'S A PICTURE OF ONE.

"My two story house is an easy walk away. I'll bring the chocolate chips for the cookies. See you there!" said _____.

3. Answer these questions.

At whose house will the baking take place? _____

Who is bringing flour and sugar? _____

Who will go over a bridge to get to the baking party? _____

Who is bringing the eggs? _____

Who is bringing the chocolate chips? _____

4. Draw the path each person might walk. Use a different color marker for each.

A THREE-PERSON DRAWING

You need:

- ☐ Two friends
- ☐ Three pieces of drawing paper (8 1/2" x 11")
- ☐ Three pencils or markers

✂ To make a cooperative drawing:

1. Explain that each person will draw only one third of each picture and no one will see what the others have drawn until all the pictures are completed.

2. Give each person a piece of paper and have him or her fold the paper into three equal sections. Open the paper so the fold lines can be seen.

3. Each person is to draw the head of a person on the top section of the paper, and then draw two lines over the fold line to show where the neck is.

4. When the head drawing is complete, fold back the top portion of the paper so only the neck lines are seen as shown in illustration two.

5. Exchange papers.

6. Draw the body in the middle section of the paper. Connect the body with the neck lines at the fold. DO NOT look at the head drawing that is folded back.

7. After drawing the body, draw lines over the next fold line to show where the legs should begin.

8. Fold back the middle section and exchange papers again.

9. Draw legs and feet on the bottom third of the paper WITHOUT looking at the other sections.

10. When everyone has completed the third drawing, take turns opening up the drawings and see what you have made.

The underlined words from Colossians 3:23 and 24 are hidden in this group of letters. The words may be forward, backward, upside down, or written at an angle.

✎ **Circle each word as you find it in the word search.**

Whatever you do, work at it with all your heart, as working for the Lord, not for men, since you know that you will receive an inheritance from the Lord as a reward. It is the Lord Christ you are serving.

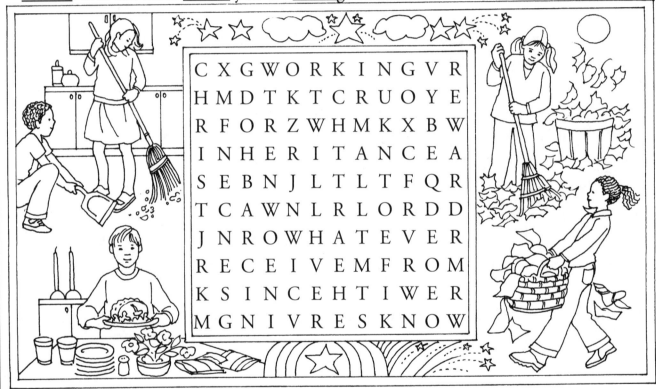

C X G W O R K I N G V R
H M D T K T C R U O Y E
R F O R Z W H M K X B W
I N H E R I T A N C E A
S E B N J L T L T F Q R
T C A W N L R L O R D D
J N R O W H A T E V E R
R E C E I V E M F R O M
K S I N C E H T I W E R
M G N I V R E S K N O W

✎ **Make a new word search and have a friend, a brother or a sister solve it for you. Hide these underlined words in your puzzle and then add letters in between the words to hide them.** The first word is written in for you.

"Whatever you do, work at it with all your heart. It is the Lord Christ you are serving."
Colossians 3:23, 24.

	W	H	A	T	E	V	E	R		

A PEOPLE SEARCH

It's fun to know about other people and to do things together with them.

✎ **Find someone you know who fits each of the descriptions in the boxes below. Ask that person to write his or her name in the box or you can draw something about that person.**

LET'S DESIGN A FROG SEARCH. DO WE KNOW ANY PURPLE FROGS?

I THINK I SAW A NEIGHBOR WITH POLKA DOTS. WILL THAT DO?

Who has blue eyes?	Who has black hair?	Who likes to sing?
Who has a fish for a pet?	Whose name has an "r" in it?	Who has a black Bible?
Who doesn't like chocolate ice cream?	Who plays football?	Who has three sisters?

One of the fun things about cooperating is

_____

HOW MANY WAYS TO BE COOPERATIVE?

✏️ **Finish the picture if the people are helping someone and working together. Put an X on the picture if they are not cooperating.**

HEY, FRED, PART OF ME IS MISSING. WILL YOU BE COOPERATIVE AND DRAW THE REST OF ME IN?

SURE! BUT I THINK I'LL GIVE YOU DIFFERENT LEGS.

A COOPERATIVE POPCORN PARTY

✎ **Ask two or more friends to join you for a popcorn party. Plan the place and date together. Then decide who should bring which items so everyone has a part in the preparation for the party.**

You need:
- ☐ Hot air popcorn popper, one or more
- ☐ Unpopped popcorn
- ☐ Paper cups, one per person
- ☐ Napkins
- ☐ Clean bed sheet

Optional:
- ☐ Salt shaker
- ☐ Parmesan cheese shaker

✂ **To make the popcorn:**

1. Spread the sheet on the floor, being careful not to step on it. Put the popcorn popper near the middle of the sheet so the popped corn will fall on the clean sheet.

2. Give each person a cup to catch popped corn in and have them sit around the edge of the sheet no closer than arm's reach from the popper.

3. Put the popcorn into the popper and turn it on. If desired, remove the top dispenser from the popper so the popped corn will pop out in all directions instead of just one.

4. As the corn pops, catch it in your cup until your cup is full. Let the other popcorn fall to the sheet.

5. If desired, sprinkle Parmesan cheese on your popped corn, and eat it!

A Cooperative Story

As you are eating your popcorn make up a story. ✎ **You start telling the story then point to someone in the group to continue it. Go around the group until everyone has had a chance to add to the story. No telling what the story will be about when you finish!**

WORKING TOGETHER EVERYWHERE

✎ **Follow the dots to see who is being cooperative at home.**

YOU CAN PAY FOR THE PIZZA AND I CAN EAT IT.

THAT'S NOT COOPERATING! LET'S PAY FOR IT TOGETHER AND EAT IT TOGETHER. I WANT TO EAT MY OWN HALF.

What are other ways you can be cooperative? ✎ **Write your answers.**

AT SCHOOL I can be cooperative by

_____

_____

AT CHURCH I can be cooperative by

_____

_____

WHAT DO YOU THINK ABOUT COOPERATING?

How can you cooperate with others when you play together?

✎ **Read these stories. Decide if the people are being cooperative or contentious. Then draw this picture ☺ beside the items that illustrate a cooperative attitude and draw this one ☹ by the items that don't.**

"CONTENTIOUS" MEANS NOT WANTING TO GET ALONG OR COOPERATE WITH OTHERS.

☐ The fifth grade class was making a float for the annual Christmas parade. Jill was not sure what to do. Susan noticed and said, "Hi, Jill. Would you like some help?"

☐ Nancy notices Donald is having a hard time getting the raked leaves into the garbage bag. She walks over and says, "Here, let me hold the bag while you put the leaves in."

☐ Doug is in the garage trying to get his baseball glove down from the hook his dad put it on, but he can't quite reach it. As his big sister Beth walks by he asks for her help. Beth answers, "I don't have time to help you get it, I'm playing with my friends right now."

✎ **Circle YES or NO to show if these kids have a cooperative attitude.**

YES NO John: "I do my part whenever I can."

YES NO Susan: "I can order the other people around."

YES NO Jason: "I try to be sure that I'm the one who does the fun parts."

YES NO Sam: "I tell the others they are doing it all wrong if they don't do it the way I want them to."

YES NO Anne: "I offer my help to someone if they need to know how to do something."

The Believers Share Responsibilities

Acts 6:1-7; 2 Timothy 4:9-13; Romans 16:1,2; Titus 3:13,14

In those days when the number of disciples was increasing, the Grecian Jews among them complained against the Hebraic Jews because their widows were being overlooked in the daily distribution of food. So the Twelve gathered all the disciples together and said, "It would not be right for us to neglect the ministry of the word of God in order to wait on tables. Brothers, choose seven men from among you who are known to be full of the Spirit and wisdom. We will turn this responsibility over to them and will give our attention to prayer and the ministry of the word."

This proposal pleased the whole group. They chose Stephen, a man full of faith and of the Holy Spirit; also Philip, Procorus, Nicanor, Timon, Parmenas, and Nicolas from Antioch, a convert to Judaism. They presented these men to the apostles, who prayed and laid their hands on them.

(Read the rest of the story on page 19)

The twelve disciples said, "Some of our work isn't getting done. We have too much to do. We need to have help. Let's ask some other people to cooperate with us." Seven men were asked to help with giving food for those who needed it.

✎ **Look in the Bible story for the names of the new helpers. Add the missing vowels (A,E,I,O,U) to the names.**

The new helpers were named:

1. S T __ P H __ N   5. T __ M __ N

2. P H __ L __ P   6. P __ R M __ N __ S

3. P R __ C __ R __ S   7. N __ C __ L __ S

4. N __ C __ N __ R

THE BIBLE TELLS ABOUT BEING COOPERATIVE

The Believers Share Responsibilities

In his letters, Paul writes about ways the people can be cooperative.

(Acts 6:1-7; 2 Timothy 4:9-13; Romans 16:1, 2; Titus 3:13, 14 continued from page 18)

[Timothy,] do your best to come to me quickly, . . . Only Luke is with me. Get Mark and bring him with you, because he is helpful to me in my ministry. I sent Tychicus to Ephesus. When you come, bring the cloak that I left with Carpus at Troas, and my scrolls, especially the parchments.

I commend to you our sister Phoebe, a servant of the church in Cenchrea. I ask you . . . to give her any help she may need from you, for she has been a great help to many people, including me.

Do everything you can to help Zenas the lawyer and Apollos on their way and see that they have everything they need. Our people must learn to devote themselves to doing what is good, in order that they may provide for daily necessities and not live unproductive lives.

✎ **Eight things are hidden in this picture. To find them, use these clues about the people who are cooperating with each other. You may find more than one of some items.**

1. Timothy and Mark are taking a **cloak** (coat) and **scrolls** to Paul. Luke is already with Paul helping him.

2. Phoebe is helping people in a **church** in Cenchrea, and the people are helping her.

3. Zenas and Apollos are packing a **trunk** for their trip. They may need to take a lot of **food** with them.

Here are some of the people from the Bible story who were cooperating when help was needed.

✎ **Follow the maze to find cooperative people. Draw yourself in the empty circle.**

Timothy Mark Luke Tychicus Phoebe Zenas

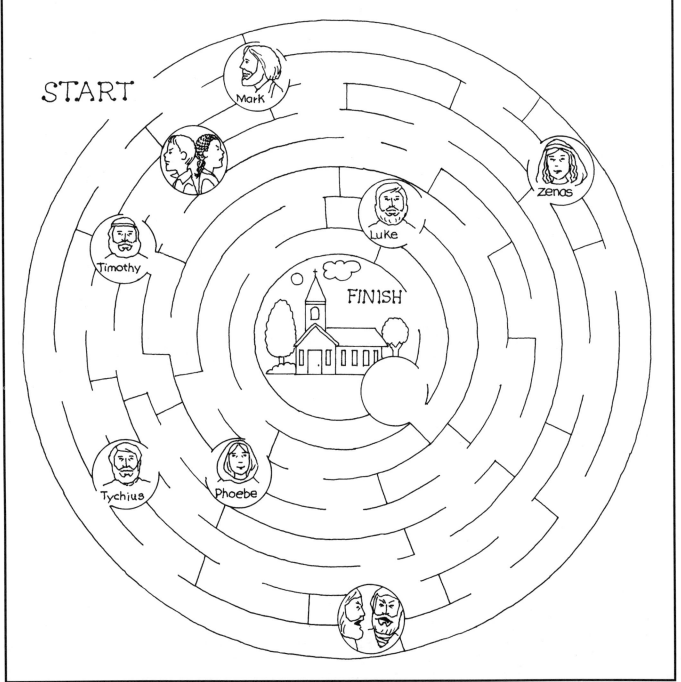

IT'S GREAT TO COOPERATE

Have an "It's Great to Cooperate" game day or night at your house. Use only those games that require cooperation. Here are some suggestions:

Musical Chairs
You need:
- [ ] Chairs
- [ ] Music

Play just like you would musical chairs except that no one is ever eliminated. Each time you remove a chair encourage your friends to try to fit onto the remaining chairs. When there is only one chair left, you'll enjoy seeing how each person gets at least some of their body on the chair, even if it is just a fingertip!

Where's the Treat?
You need:
- [ ] Clue words
- [ ] Hidden treats
- [ ] A parent or older brother/sister

Before your friends arrive have your parent or an older brother or sister hide the treats and make up one long clue to help find them. The clue could then be cut up so that one word is on each piece of paper. Hide the pieces of paper. When your friends arrive, hunt for the clue words, put them all together, then enjoy the hidden treats!

Toss Across
You need:
- [ ] Ping pong balls
- [ ] Paper cups

Divide your friends up into pairs. Have the pairs stand facing one another and give each person a paper cup. Hand a ping pong ball to each pair then have a contest to see which pair can successfully toss and catch the ping pong ball in the cups the most times or from the farthest distance.

Let's work together on this page.

✎ **Figure out the code. Then have a friend decode the verse.**

0 = A	____ = F	____ = K	____ = Q	42 = V
2 = B	____ = G	____ = L	____ = R	44 = W
4 = C	____ = H	____ = M	____ = S	46 = X
6 = D	____ = I	____ = N	____ = T	48 = Y
8 = E	____ = J	____ = O	____ = U	50 = Z
			____ = P	

A CRYPTOGRAPHER?

THAT'S SOMEONE WHO THINKS UP A CODE OR FIGURES ONE OUT.

MUST BE A PUZZLING PERSON!

Ephesians 4:16

From __ __ __ , [__ __ __] the __ __ __ __ body, [the __ __ __ __ __ __]
    14-16-24   [12-28-6]   44-14-28-22-8   4-14-40-34-4-14

__ __ __ __ __ __ and held __ __ __ __ __ __ __ __ by every
18-28-16-26-8-6   38-28-12-8-38-14-8-34

__ __ __ __ __ __ __ __ __ __ __ ligament, __ __ __ __ __ and
36-40-30-30-28-34-38-16-26-12   12-34-28-44-36

__ __ __ __ __ __ itself up in __ __ __ __ , as each part
2-40-16-22-6-36   22-28-42-8

does its __ __ __ __ .
       44-28-34-20

THE VALUE OF
BEING COOPERATIVE

HOW CAN YOU KNOW WHAT YOUR VALUES ARE?

Look at the things you DO, SAY, and THINK. If you spend time doing something, then you know it is one of your values.

✎ **Draw a picture of yourself here. Are you thinking what is in the thought balloon?**

God's values are the STANDARD to help me know how to live my life and treat other people

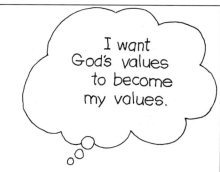

I want God's values to become my values.

My name is _____ .

Being cooperative _____ important to me.
is   is not

I _____ spend time doing things with other people.
do   do not

Being willing to do something with others is being cooperative.

I can show that being cooperative is becoming my value when I_____
_____and _____.

✂ **Design and fill in these cooperative coupons. Give them to members of your family or friends.**

Cooperative Coupon
Name_____
Date_____
I'd like to cooperate with you by _____ _____.

Cooperative Coupon
Name_____
Date_____
I'd like to cooperate with you by _____ _____.

WHAT IS BEING HUMBLE?

BEING HUMBLE IS . . .
knowing you are not better than other people.

I think being humble also means _____

_____

These kids are thinking thoughts that help them be humble.

✎ **Write a thought in the empty thought balloon.**

Being humble is important to me.

When I am careful not to put myself above others and I put others first, then being humble becomes one of my values.

Name _____

Date _____

God's values are the STANDARD to help me know how to live my life and treat other people

THE BIBLE TELLS ABOUT BEING HUMBLE

A Humble Centurion Believes in Jesus

Luke 7:1-10

When Jesus had finished saying all this in the hearing of the people, he entered Capernaum. There a centurion's servant, whom his master valued highly, was sick and about to die. The centurion heard of Jesus and sent some elders of the Jews to him, asking him to come and heal his servant. When they came to Jesus, they pleaded earnestly with him, "This man deserves to have you do this, because he loves our nation and has built our synagogue." So Jesus went with them.

(Read the rest of this story on page 26)

✎ **Unscramble the words to fill in the blanks. Use the Bible story above for help.**

1. The centurion's _____ was sick.
   vtnsaer

2. The _____ knew Jesus could heal him.
   nnrctiuoe

3. Some _____ went to ask Jesus to _____ to the house.
   eerdls   mceo

4. _____ went with the elders.
   ssJue

✎ **Put check marks by the sentences that show the centurion was humble.**

_____ He didn't think he was more important than the other people.

_____ He didn't think he deserved special attention.

_____ He thought Jesus should follow his orders.

_____ He thought he was more important than his friends.

THE BIBLE TELLS ABOUT BEING HUMBLE

A Humble Centurion Believes in Jesus

(Luke 7:1-10 continued from page 25)
He was not far from the house when the centurion sent friends to say to him: "Lord, don't trouble yourself, for I do not deserve to have you come under my roof. That is why I did not even consider myself worthy to come to you. But say the word, and my servant will be healed. For I myself am a man under authority, with soldiers under me. I tell this one, 'Go,' and he goes; and that one, 'Come,' and he comes. I say to my servant, 'Do this,' and he does it."

When Jesus heard this, he was amazed at him, and turning to the crowd following him, he said, "I tell you, I have not found such great faith even in Israel." Then the men who had been sent returned to the house and found the servant well.

✎ **Read the rebus story. Draw in the missing pictures.**

 came to the town of Capernaum. The

Jesus   centurion's

"REBUS" MEANS USING A PICTURE IN PLACE OF A WORD.

 was so sick the was going to die.

servant

The asked some to go get to heal the [   ] .

elders

 went with the to the [   ] house.

Then the sent to tell not to come.

friends

The was a humble man and didn't want to bother .

The said that the knew that

could heal the without coming to the house.

When the and the came back, the was healed!

PUPPETS FOR A PLAY
ABOUT BEING HUMBLE

✎ **To make puppets and background scenes, decorate and cut out the puppet pieces and background scenes on these two pages. Use the puppets with the puppet play on page 30. You may want to cover the puppets with clear plastic adhesive to make them sturdier and help them last longer. Use a clothespin to "clip" each face on the tab below the face. Stand up the clothespin and attach the clothes to the front as shown.**

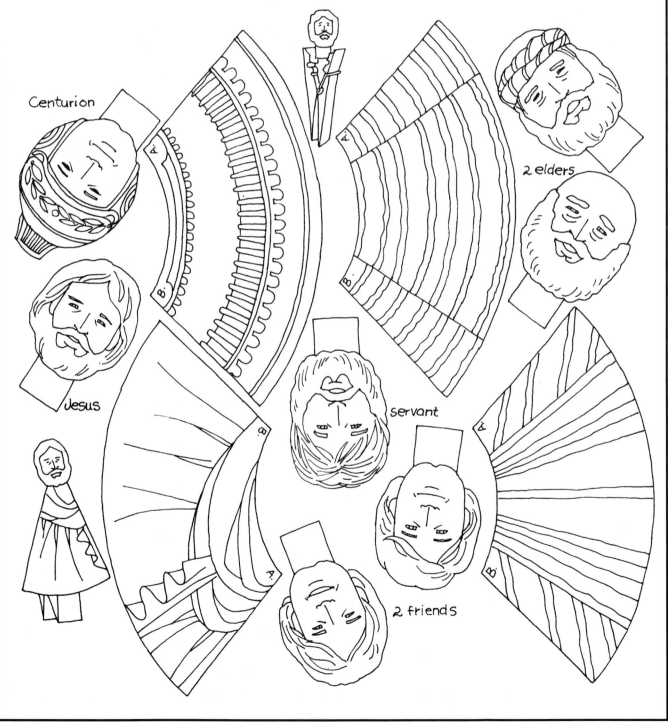

PUPPETS FOR A PLAY
ABOUT BEING HUMBLE

THE CENTURION IS HUMBLE

A puppet play based on Matthew 7:1-10

The people in this exciting true event are: Jesus, a centurion, a servant, two elders, two friends, and a crowd of listeners

PREPARATION: Follow the directions for making the puppets and background pieces on pages 28-29.

SETTING: The city of Capernaum, at and near the centurion's house.

[JESUS and the CROWD of people are on the right side. On the left is the CENTURION'S house and the CENTURION, two ELDERS, and two FRIENDS are standing around the bed of the SERVANT.]

CENTURION *(to the people around the bed)* : Our servant is so sick, I don't think he can live much longer. I want to help him get well. *(turns to the ELDERS)* Will you please go to Jesus and ask Him to come to our house and heal my servant?

[ELDERS leave the house and go to JESUS.]

ELDER #1: Jesus, the centurion knows you can heal people and his servant is very, very sick. Would you go with us to his house? The servant has worked hard for our country and our church and the centurion wants you to heal his servant.

[JESUS and the ELDERS start walking toward the CENTURION'S house, while the crowd follows slowly behind them. At the house, the CENTURION turns to the FRIENDS.]

CENTURION: I don't want Jesus to have to come all the way to my house. He does a lot of teaching and helping so many people. I don't deserve to have such an important person come to my house, and I'm not important enough to go to Him and stand before Him.

FRIEND #1: But, Sir, you are a very important man yourself. When you tell the soldiers to do things, they have to do them even if they don't want to. You are in charge of many servants and they obey you. Why shouldn't you just tell Jesus what to do even if it causes him trouble?

CENTURION: I want to be as kind and thoughtful to Jesus as I am to everyone else. Even though I have lots of people who follow my instructions, I am not more important than they are. But Jesus is more important. He is God's Son!

FRIEND #2: But Jesus is already coming. It is probably too late to stop him.

CENTURION: Will both of you go and see if you can stop him from going to any more trouble for me? Please ask Him to just say the word and I know my servant will be healed.

[FRIENDS leave the house, meet JESUS with the ELDERS, and the CROWD, and give JESUS the message.]

JESUS *(to the crowd)* : The centurion knows that I can heal without going to his house. It is wonderful that he has such great faith in me. I will heal his servant.

[FRIENDS and ELDERS leave while JESUS is talking to the CROWD and go back to the house. The SERVANT is standing up.]

CENTURION *(to SERVANT)*: I'm glad I asked Jesus to heal you. This is a special day for all of us.

GOD HELPS THE HUMBLE

Psalm 25:9 tells about being humble.

✎ **Solve the crossword puzzle to finish the Bible verse.**

ACROSS

1. not wrong

2. not thinking you are more important than others is being _____.

3. One who made everything

DOWN

4. helps someone learn something

5. shows the way to go

He, [_____] , _____ the
(3 across)   (5 down)

_____ in what is _____ and
(2 across)   (1 across)

_____ them his way.
(4 across)

GOD LIKES US TO BE HUMBLE.

THAT HONORS HIM INSTEAD OF OURSELVES.

✎ **Finish these sentences by decoding the words.** Write the alphabet letter that comes before each letter shown. The first few letters are done for you.

When you are humble, GOD helps you know what is the

s j h i u   u i j o h   u p   e p

r i g ___ ___ ___ ___ ___ ___ ___ ___ .

And GOD teaches you His way to

m j w f   z p v s   m j g f   b o e   u s f b u   p u i f s t

l i ___ ___ ___ ___ ___ ___ ___ ___ ___ ___ .

GOD LOVES EVERYONE THE SAME

While every person is unique, we are all alike in many ways. God loves all people just the same—with all His heart!

✎ **Draw lines to match the ones that are alike.**

✎ **Unscramble the words and finish the sentence.**

I want to think about _____ kids and how I can _____ something
                             rtoeh   od

with or _____ them, instead of just thinking about _____.
     rof   syfeml

A HUMBLE PERSON

✎ **Draw a self portrait and answer the questions below.**

1. What is your favorite thing to do when you have extra time? _____
_____

2. What is your least favorite thing to do? ___
_____

3. What are three ways you are different from the other people you know?_____
_____
_____
_____

ME

4. What are three ways you are the same as people you know?

_____
_____
_____

I am a special person, made by God. Other people are also special because God made them that way.

When I am a humble person,

I do not make _____ of _____ _____ .
               nuf   rehto   elpoep

I do not think that _____ are _____ important than I _____ .
                  srehto   ssel   ma

A MAZE ABOUT BEING HUMBLE

✏ **Follow the line through each set of shapes. When you come to a letter write it on the line at the bottom of the page. The first letter is done for you.**

BEING HUMBLE IS

T̲ __ __ __ __ __ __ __ __ of

__ __ __ __ __ __ __ more than yourself, and

__ __ __ being too __ __ __ __ __ of yourself.

HAUGHTY OR HUMBLE?

To BE "HAUGHTY" MEANS TO THINK YOU ARE BETTER THAN EVERYONE ELSE.

IT'S THE OPPOSITE OF "HUMBLE."

Humble

Haughty

✎ **Read the situations below. Decide whether the response is a Haughty one or a Humble one. Circle the appropriate picture. If you circle the Haughty face write what a Humble response might have been.**

Humble

Haughty

It's easy for me to do my homework and turn it in on time. I like doing it. Jonathan never does his homework; he is too lazy. I'm better than Jonathan.

_____

_____

Humble

Haughty

I like being on the soccer team. It's great when we win and I help the team a lot. We all work together, even the kids who can't play as well. You can tell they are doing their best.

_____

_____

Humble

Haughty

Jackie doesn't know that I'm the best kid in math. I even won the school award last week. He is so dumb in math; I'll tell him how good I am.

_____

_____

Humble

Haughty

I can tell Elise is thirsty after that long ball game. I'm next in line at the water fountain, but I'll let her go ahead of me.

_____

_____

John the Baptist and Jesus

Matthew 3:1-17

In those days John the Baptist came, preaching in the Desert of Judea. . . . People went out to him from Jerusalem and all Judea and the whole region of the Jordan. Confessing their sins, they were baptized by him in the Jordan River.

But when he saw many of the Pharisees and Sadducees coming to where he was baptizing, he said to them: . . .

"I baptize you with water for repentance. But after me will come one who is more powerful than I, whose sandals I am not fit to carry. . . ."

(Read the rest of the story on page 37)

(Read the rest of the story on page 37)

JOHN COULD HAVE TALKED ABOUT ALL THE PEOPLE WHO CAME TO HEAR HIM.

HE WAS HUMBLE. HE WANTED THE PEOPLE TO KNOW ABOUT JESUS, INSTEAD.

✎ **Draw a line from the sentence to the word(s) that complete it. Look at the Bible story above for help.**

1. People came to hear John from the city of
_____ and all _____.

2. John preached in the _____.

3. John baptized people in the _____.

4. People came to hear John from the whole region of _____.

Jordan

Jerusalem

Desert of Judea

Judea

Jordan River

THE BIBLE TELLS ABOUT BEING HUMBLE

John the Baptist and Jesus

(Matthew 3:1-17 continued from page 36)

Then Jesus came from Galilee to the Jordan to be baptized by John. But John tried to deter him, saying, "I need to be baptized by you, and do you come to me?"

Jesus replied, "Let it be so now; it is proper for us to do this to fulfill all righteousness." Then John consented.

"DETER" MEANS TO TRY TO STOP.

As soon as Jesus was baptized, he went up out of the water. At that moment heaven was opened, and he saw the Spirit of God descending like a dove and lighting on him. And a voice from heaven said, "This is my Son, whom I love; with him I am well pleased."

"CONSENTED" MEANS HE SAID OK.

✏️ **To find out how John showed humility, fix the spacing in this paragraph. The first few words are done for you.**

Joh n/the Bap tist/ba ptized peo plew hen the y confe s sedthe ir s in s.Johnwa s hum blew hen hes aid Je susis m or eim port ant than I am.Jes us as ked Jo hnto bap tiz e hi m.Johntri edtos ay 'No' toJe sus, andJe sussa idit wasim port antf or Himto doth is. Wh enJoh n ba ptiz edJ e sus Gods poke fro mhea ve nandsa idth at Jes uswa s Hi sSo n.

Lots of hhhhhhhhhhhs and mmmmmmmmms are mixed up in this Bible verse.
✎ **Read each word carefully and cross out only the extra "h" and "m" letters to read what the Bible says in Romans 12:16 about being humble. Then do the same thing for the fill-in-the-blank sentences.**

Romans 12:16

mLimve hinh harmmmonmy mwithhh monmeh anmothherm.

hDoh nmot hhbem prommudh,

bhuth bemm mwillhming toh masshhociahte mwithh

peommpleh ofhh mlomw pomsihtion.

Dohm mnoth bhe conmceithedh.

1. When you get along with others you _____ in _____ .
   mlimve
   harmmmonmy

"HARMONY" MEANS BEING TOGETHER IN PEACE. IT ALSO MEANS MUSIC WITH NOTES THAT SOUND GREAT TOGETHER. BUT WOULD YOU SAVE YOUR HARMONY FOR THE DEEP WOODS PLEASE?

2. When you are friends with someone who has less than you do, you _____ with _____ of low _____ .
   masshhociahte   peommpleh   pomsihtion

3. Thinking you are better than you really are is being _____ or _____ .
   prommudh   conmceithedh

JOHN THE BAPTIST BOOKMARK

You need:
- ☐ Ribbon
- ☐ Glue
- ☐ Scissors
- ☐ Pencils or markers

✂ **To make a John the Baptist Bookmark:**

1. Trace then decorate the John the Baptist figure below.
2. Print the first part of the Bible verse from page 38 on the figure.
3. Cut out figure and glue to a ribbon.

"Live in harmony with one another" Romans 12:16

✎ **Use the code to finish this official document.**

CODE BOX

= A ● = E (I symbol) = I (O symbol) = O (U symbol) =U

Official Document of Humble Intentions

When I am humble,

I will l __(E)__ __(A)__ r n from the B __(I)__ b l __(E)__ about how God says to live

and treat other people.

I will l __(I)__ s t __(E)__ n instead of doing all the t __(A)__ l k __(I)__ n g.

I can be c __(O)__ r r __(E)__ c t __(E)__ d when I make a m __(I)__ s t __(A)__ k __(E)__ .

(I don't always have to be right.)

I am willing to do __(E)__ __(A)__ s y (even boring) tasks that need to be done.

(I don't always need to be the one to do the important things)

I will try to d __(O)__ something very h __(A)__ r d without

being angry or talking back. _____

Signature

THINK ABOUT OTHERS

✎ **Draw an object or animal in the box whose name begins with the letter above the box. Then fill in the blanks by writing the first letter of each object.**

WHEN I AM

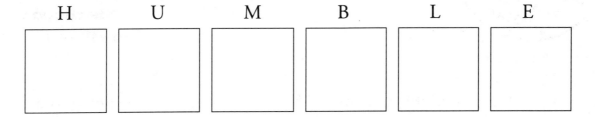

H   U   M   B   L   E

I think about

_____ _____ _____ _____ _____ _____

more than I think about

_____ _____ _____ _____ _____ _____ .

I am not

_____ _____ _____ _____ _____ _____ _____ .

WHY AREN'T THERE ANY FROGS ON THIS PAGE?

WHAT DO YOU MEAN? WE'RE HERE AREN'T WE?

THE VALUE OF BEING HUMBLE

God's values are the STANDARD to help me know how to live my life and treat other people

I want God's values to become my values.

✎ **Draw a picture of yourself here. Are you thinking what is in the thought balloon?**

How can you know what your values are?
Look at the things you DO, SAY, and THINK. If you spend time doing something, then you know it is one of your values.

My name is _____.

Being humble _____ important to me. I _____ spend
　　　　　　　　　　is　is not　　　　　　　　　　　　do　do not
time thinking about other people instead of just myself.

Knowing I am not more important than other people is being humble.

I can show that being humble is becoming my value when I _____

and _____ .

✎ **In the space below, design an award for being humble. Cut it out and present it to someone you know who is a good example of being humble.**

VALUE BUILDERS SERIES INDEX
BY VALUE

Accepting
Romans 15:7
Galatians 3:28
Luke 7 — Jesus and the woman with no name
Acts 10 — Peter's vision and visit

Appreciative
See thankful

Attentive
Psalm 34:15
James 1:19
Nehemiah 8 — Ezra reads the law
Luke 10 — Mary listens to Jesus

Caring
See concerned

Choices
See wise

Committed
1 Kings 8:61
Proverbs 16:3
Esther 4 — Esther
John 1 — Andrew follows Jesus

Compassionate
2 Corinthians 1:3-4
1 Peter 3:8
Luke 10 — Good Samaritan
Luke 23 — Jesus on the cross

Concerned
1 Corinthians 12:25
1 John 3:17
Matthew 25 — Jesus teaches to meet needs
Acts 2 — Church provides for each other

Confident
Philippians 4:13
Psalm 139:14
1 Samuel 17 — David and Goliath
Nehemiah 6 — Nehemiah isn't intimidated

Considerate
See respectful, kind

Consistent
1 John 3:18
Psalm 33:4
Matthew 26 — Jesus in the garden
Daniel 6 — Daniel as administrator

Contented
See peaceful

Conviction
Deuteronomy 13:6-8
Acts 4:19-20
Daniel 3 — Blazing furnace and three Hebrews
John 2 — Jesus clears the temple courts

Cooperative
Colossians 3:23-24
Ephesians 4:16
Acts 6 — Disciples share responsibilities
Exodus 18 — Jethro gives Moses a plan

Courageous
Joshua 1:9
Isaiah 41:10
Acts 23 — Paul's nephew
Esther 4 — Esther

Creative
See resourceful

Decision Making
See purposeful

Dedicated
See committed

Dependable
See responsible

Diligent
See persevering, purposeful, responsible

Discerning
See wise

Discipleship
See teachable, prayerful, worshipful, faith, holy

Discipline
See self-disciplined

Empathy
Galatians 6:2
Hebrews 13:3
John 11 — Jesus at Lazarus's death
1 Samuel 19 — Jonathan speaks up for David

Endurance
See persevering, self-disciplined, purposeful

Enthusiasm
See joyful

Fairness
Leviticus 19:15
Romans 12:17
James 2 — Favoritism at a meeting
Matthew 20 — Parable of workers

Faith
John 3:16
Hebrews 11:6
Acts 16 — Philippian jailer
Matthew 8 — Centurion sends servant to Jesus

Faithful
See loyal

VALUE BUILDERS SERIES INDEX
BY VALUE

Fellowship
See friendly

Flexibility
See cooperative, initiative, resourceful

Forgiving
Ephesians 4:32
Leviticus 19:18
Matthew 18   Parable of unforgiving servant
Genesis 45   Joseph forgives brothers

Friendly
Luke 6:31
Proverbs 17:17
1 Samuel 18   David and Jonathan
Acts 9   Paul and Barnabas

Generosity
Matthew 5:42
Hebrews 13:16
Ruth 2   Boaz gives grain to Ruth
2 Corinthians 8   Paul's letter about sharing

Gentle
Matthew 11:29-30
Philippians 4:5
Mark 10   Jesus and the children
John 19   Joseph of Arimathea prepares Jesus' body

Genuineness
See sincerity

Giving
See generosity

Goodness
See consistent, holy

Helpfulness
Acts 20:35
Ephesians 6:7-8
Exodus 2   Miriam and baby Moses
Mark 14   Disciples prepare Last Supper

Holy
I Peter 1:15
Psalm 51:10
Acts 10   Cornelius
Exodus 3   Moses and the burning bush

Honest
Leviticus 19:11
Ephesians 4:25
Mark 14   Peter lies about knowing Jesus
1 Samuel 3   Samuel tells Eli the truth

Honor
See obedient, respectful, reverence

Hopeful
Jeremiah 29:11
Romans 15:13
Acts 1   Jesus will return/Ascension
Genesis 15   Abraham looks to the future

Humble
Psalm 25:9
Romans 12:16
Luke 7   Centurion asks Jesus to heal son
Matthew 3   John the Baptist and Jesus

Independent
See confident, initiative

Initiative
Joshua 22:5
Ephesians 4:29
John 13   Jesus washes feet
Nehemiah 2   Nehemiah asks to go to Jerusalem

Integrity
See consistent, holy, honest

Joyful
1 Thessalonians 5:16
1 Peter 1:8
Luke 2   Jesus' birth
Acts 12   Rhoda greets Peter

Justice
See fairness

Kind
1 Thessalonians 5:15
Luke 6:35
2 Samuel 9   David and Mephibosheth
Acts 28   Malta islanders and Paul

Knowledge
See teachable

Listening
See attentive

Long suffering
See patience

Loving
John 13:34-35
1 Corinthians 13:4-7
Luke 15   Prodigal son
John 11   Mary, Martha, Lazarus and Jesus

Loyal
1 Chronicles 29:18
Romans 12:5
1 Samuel 20   David and Jonathan
Ruth 1   Ruth and Naomi

Meek
See gentle, humble

VALUE BUILDERS SERIES INDEX
BY VALUE

Merciful
Psalm 103:10
Micah 6:8
1 Samuel 25   Abigail helps David show mercy
Matthew 18   Unmerciful servant

Obedient
See also respectful
1 Samuel 15:22
Ephesians 6:1
1 Samuel 17   David takes lunch
Acts 9   Ananias at Saul's conversion

Patience
Psalm 37: 7
Ephesians 4:2
Genesis 26   Isaac opens new wells
Nehemiah 6   Nehemiah stands firm

Peaceful
John 14:27
Hebrews 13:5-6
Acts 12   Peter sleeping in prison
Matthew 6   Jesus teaches contentment

Peer pressure, response to
See confident, conviction, wise

Persevering
Galatians 6:9
James 1:2-3
Acts 27   Paul in shipwreck
Exodus 5   Moses doesn't give up

Praise
See prayerful, thankful, worshipful

Prayerful
Philippians 4:6
James 5:16
Luke 11   Jesus teaches disciples
Daniel 6   Daniel prays daily

Pure
See holy

Purposeful
James 1:22
1 Corinthians 15:58
Matthew 26   Jesus in Gethsemane
Joshua 24   Joshua serves God

Reliable
See responsible

Repentant
Acts 26:20
1 John 1:9
Luke 15   Prodigal son
Luke 22   Peter's denial

Resourceful
Philippians 4:9
1 Peter 4:10
Luke 5   Man lowered through roof
Luke 19   Zacchaeus

Respectful
Deuteronomy 5:16
1 Peter 2:17
1 Samuel 26   David doesn't kill Saul
Acts 16   Lydia and other believers

Responsible
Galatians 6:4-5
Proverbs 20:11
Acts 20   Paul continues his work
Numbers 13   Caleb follows instructions

Reverence
Daniel 6:26-27
Psalm 78:4, 7
Daniel 3   Blazing furnace and three Hebrews
Matthew 21   Triumphal entry

Self-controlled
See self-disciplined

Self-disciplined
1 Timothy 4:7-8
2 Timothy 1:7
Daniel 1   Daniel and king's meat
John 19   Jesus was mocked

Self-esteem
See confident

Sensitivity
See empathy, compassionate, concerned, kind

Service (servanthood)
See cooperative, generosity, helpful, stewardship

Sharing
See generosity, stewardship

Sincerity
Romans 12:9
Job 33:3
Mark 5   Jairus and his daughter
2 Timothy 1   Timothy

Stewardship
Luke 3:11
Ephesians 5:15-16
2 Chronicles 31   Temple contributions
Acts 4   Believers share

Submission
See humble, respectful, self-disciplined

Supportive
See friendly, loving

Sympathy
See compassionate, concerned

Teachable
Joshua 1:8
Psalm 32:8
Luke 2 — Young Jesus in the temple
Acts 18 — Apollos with Priscilla and Aquila

Thankful
Psalm 28:17
Colossians 3:17
1 Chronicles 29 — Celebrating the temple
Romans 16 — Paul thanks Phoebe, Priscilla and Aquila

Tolerant
See accepting

Trusting
Proverbs 3:5-6
Psalm 9:10
Acts 27 — Sailors with Paul in shipwreck
2 Kings 18 — Hezekiah trusts God

Trustworthiness
See honest, responsible

Truthful
See honest

Unselfish
Romans 15:1-3
Philippians 2:4
Luke 23 — God gives His Son
John 6 — Boy gives lunch

Wise
Proverbs 8:10
James 3:13
1 Kings 3 — Solomon asks for wisdom
Daniel 1 — Daniel and king's meat

Worshipful
Psalm 86:12
Psalm 122:1
Nehemiah 8 — Ezra and the people worship
Acts 16 — Paul and Silas in jail

VALUE BUILDERS SERIES INDEX
BY SCRIPTURE

Genesis 15	Abraham looks to future	Hopeful
Genesis 26	Isaac opens new wells	Patience
Genesis 45	Joseph forgives brothers	Forgiving
Exodus 2	Miriam and baby Moses	Helpful
Exodus 3	Moses and the burning bush	Holy
Exodus 5	Moses doesn't give up	Persevering
Exodus 18	Jethro gives Moses a plan	Cooperative
Leviticus 19:11		Honest
Leviticus 19:15		Fairness
Leviticus 19:18		Forgiving
Numbers 13	Caleb follows instructions	Responsible
Deuteronomy 5:16		Respectful
Deuteronomy 13:6-8		Conviction
Joshua 1:8		Teachable
Joshua 1:9		Courageous
Joshua 22:5		Initiative
Joshua 24	Joshua serves God	Purposeful
Ruth 1	Ruth and Naomi	Loyal
Ruth 2	Boaz gives grain to Ruth	Generosity
1 Samuel 3	Samuel tells Eli the truth	Honest
1 Samuel 15:22		Obedient
1 Samuel 17	David and Goliath	Confident
1 Samuel 17	David takes lunch	Obedient
1 Samuel 18	David and Jonathan	Friendly
1 Samuel 19	Jonathan speaks up for David	Empathy
1 Samuel 20	David and Jonathan	Loyal
1 Samuel 25	Abigail helps David show mercy	Merciful
1 Samuel 26	David doesn't kill Saul	Respectful
2 Samuel 9	David and Mephibosheth	Kind
1 Kings 3	Solomon asks for wisdom	Wise
1 Kings 8:61		Committed
2 Kings 18	Hezekiah trusts God	Trusting
1 Chronicles 29	Celebrating the temple	Thankful
1 Chronicles 29:18		Loyal
2 Chronicles 31	Temple contributions	Stewardship
Nehemiah 2	Nehemiah asks to go to Jerusalem	Initiative
Nehemiah 6	Nehemiah isn't intimidated	Confident
Nehemiah 6	Nehemiah stands firm	Patience
Nehemiah 8	Ezra and the people worship	Worshipful
Nehemiah 8	Ezra reads the law	Attentive
Esther 4	Esther	Committed
Esther 4	Esther	Courageous
Job 33:3		Sincerity

Psalm 9:10		Trusting
Psalm 25:9		Humble
Psalm 28:17		Thankful
Psalm 32:8		Teachable
Psalm 33:4		Consistent
Psalm 34:15		Attentive
Psalm 37:7		Patience
Psalm 51:10		Holy
Psalm 78:4, 7		Reverence
Psalm 86:12		Worshipful
Psalm 103:10		Merciful
Psalm 122:1		Worshipful
Psalm 139:14		Confident
Proverbs 3:5-6		Trusting
Proverbs 8:10		Wise
Proverbs 16:3		Committed
Proverbs 17:17		Friendly
Proverbs 20:11		Responsible
Isaiah 41:10		Courageous
Jeremiah 29:11		Hopeful
Daniel 1	Daniel and king's meat	Self-disciplined
Daniel 1	Daniel and king's meat	Wise
Daniel 3	Blazing furnace and three Hebrews	Conviction
Daniel 3	Blazing furnace and three Hebrews	Reverence
Daniel 6	Daniel as administrator	Consistent
Daniel 6	Daniel prays daily	Prayerful
Daniel 6:26-27		Reverence
Micah 6:8		Merciful
Matthew 3	John the Baptist and Jesus	Humble
Matthew 5:42		Generosity
Matthew 6	Jesus teaches contentment	Peaceful
Matthew 8	Centurion sends servant to Jesus	Faith
Matthew 11:29-30		Gentle
Matthew 18	Unmerciful servant	Merciful
Matthew 18	Parable of unforgiving servant	Forgiving
Matthew 20	Parable of workers	Fairness
Matthew 21	Triumphal entry	Reverence
Matthew 25	Jesus teaches to meet needs	Concerned
Matthew 26	Jesus in Gethsemane	Purposeful
Matthew 26	Jesus in the garden	Consistent
Mark 5	Jairus and his daughter	Sincerity
Mark 10	Jesus and the children	Gentle
Mark 14	Disciples prepare Last Supper	Helpful
Mark 14	Peter lies about knowing Jesus	Honest
Luke 2	Jesus' birth	Joyful
Luke 2	Young Jesus in the temple	Teachable
Luke 3:11		Stewardship
Luke 5	Man lowered through roof	Resourceful
Luke 6:31		Friendly
Luke 6:35		Kind

VALUE BUILDERS SERIES INDEX
BY SCRIPTURE

Luke 7	Centurion asks Jesus to heal son	Humble
Luke 7	Jesus and woman with no name	Accepting
Luke 10	Good Samaritan	Compassionate
Luke 10	Mary listens to Jesus	Attentive
Luke 11	Jesus teaches disciples	Prayerful
Luke 15	Prodigal son	Loving
Luke 15	Prodigal son	Repentant
Luke 19	Zacchaeus	Resourceful
Luke 22	Peter's denial	Repentant
Luke 23	God gives His Son	Unselfish
Luke 23	Jesus on the cross	Compassionate

John 1	Andrew follows Jesus	Committed
John 2	Jesus clears the temple courts	Conviction
John 3:16		Faith
John 6	Boy gives lunch	Unselfish
John 11	Jesus at Lazarus's death	Empathy
John 11	Mary, Martha, Lazarus, and Jesus	Loving
John 13	Jesus washes feet	Initiative
John 13:34-35		Loving
John 14:27		Peaceful
John 19	Jesus was mocked	Self-disciplined
John 19	Joseph of Arimathea prepares Jesus' body	Gentle

Acts 1	Jesus will return/Ascension	Hopeful
Acts 2	Church provides for each other	Concerned
Acts 4	Believers share	Stewardship
Acts 4:19-20		Conviction
Acts 6	Disciples share responsibilities	Cooperative
Acts 9	Ananias at Saul's conversion	Obedient
Acts 9	Paul and Barnabas	Friendly
Acts 10	Cornelius	Holy
Acts 10	Peter's vision and visit	Accepting
Acts 12	Peter sleeping in prison	Peaceful
Acts 12	Rhoda greets Peter	Joyful
Acts 16	Paul and Silas in jail	Worshipful
Acts 16	Philippian jailer	Faith
Acts 16	Lydia and other believers	Respectful
Acts 18	Apollos with Priscilla and Aquila	Teachable
Acts 20	Paul continues his work	Responsible
Acts 20:35		Helpful
Acts 23	Paul's nephew	Courageous
Acts 26:20		Repentant
Acts 27	Paul in a shipwreck	Persevering
Acts 27	Sailors with Paul in shipwreck	Trusting
Acts 28	Malta islanders with Paul	Kind

Romans 12:5		Loyal
Romans 12:9		Sincerity
Romans 12:16		Humble
Romans 12:17		Fairness
Romans 15:1-3		Unselfish
Romans 15:7		Accepting
Romans 15:13		Hopeful
Romans 16	Paul thanks Phoebe, Priscilla, and Aquila	Thankful

1 Corinthians 12:25		Concerned
1 Corinthians 13:4-7		Loving
1 Corinthians 15:58		Purposeful
2 Corinthians 1:3-4		Compassionate
2 Corinthians 8	Paul's letter about sharing	Generosity
Galatians 3:28		Accepting
Galatians 6:2		Empathy
Galatians 6:4-5		Responsible
Galatians 6:9		Persevering
Ephesians 4:2		Patience
Ephesians 4:16		Cooperative
Ephesians 4:25		Honest
Ephesians 4:29		Initiative
Ephesians 4:32		Forgiving
Ephesians 5:15-16		Stewardship
Ephesians 6:1		Obedient
Ephesians 6:7-8		Helpful
Philippians 2:4		Unselfish
Philippians 4:5		Gentle
Philippians 4:6		Prayerful
Philippians 4:9		Resourceful
Philippians 4:13		Confident
Colossians 3:17		Thankful
Colossians 3:23-24		Cooperative
1 Thessalonians 5:15		Kind
1 Thessalonians 5:16		Joyful
1 Timothy 4:7-8		Self-disciplined
2 Timothy 1	Timothy	Sincerity
2 Timothy 1:7		Self-disciplined
Hebrews 11:6		Faith
Hebrews 13:3		Empathy
Hebrews 13:5-6		Peaceful
Hebrews 13:16		Generosity
James 1:2-3		Persevering
James 1:19		Attentive
James 1:22		Purposeful
James 2	Favoritism at a meeting	Fairness
James 3:13		Wise
James 5:16		Prayerful
1 Peter 1:8		Joyful
1 Peter 1:15		Holy
1 Peter 2:17		Respectful
1 Peter 3:8		Compassionate
1 Peter 4:10		Resourceful
1 John 1:9		Repentant
1 John 3:17		Concerned
1 John 3:18		Consistent